how to train your dog

ISBN 0-87666-284-X

The author with two of his fully trained, imported, German Shepherd Dogs.

how to TRAIN YOUR DOG

by

Ernest H. Hart

book #1   basic training

photographs by the author
and by Louise Van der Meid

Distributed in the U.S.A. by T.F.H. Publications, Inc., 211 West Sylvania Avenue, P.O. Box 27, Neptune City, N.J. 07753; in England by T.F.H. (Gt. Britain) Ltd., 13 Nutley Lane, Reigate, Surrey; in Canada to the book store and library trade by Clarke, Irwin & Company, Clarwin House, 791 St. Clair Avenue West, Toronto 10, Ontario; in Canada to the pet trade by Rolf C. Hagen Ltd., 3225 Sartelon Street, Montreal 382, Quebec; in Southeast Asia by Y.W. Ong, 9 Lorong 36 Geylang, Singapore 14; in Australia and the south Pacific by Pet Imports Pty. Ltd., P.O. Box 149, Brookvale 2100, N.S.W., Australia. Published by T.F.H. Publications, Inc. Ltd., The British Crown Colony of Hong Kong.

A silent token of my
esteem; I dedicate this book

to
Merle

how to train your dog

CONTENTS

The epitome of training to aid mankind . . .
Barry, the St. Bernard, one of the most
famous dogs of modern times. Trained to
search out and find people trapped by the
many avalanches that plunge down from the
snowy Alpine heights, he saved the lives of
forty persons from frozen death. Barry is
seen here with his master before the historic
steps of the St. Bernard monastery.

CHAPTER 1

PROLOGUE TO TRAINING

The purpose of this book is to train you to train your dog in the quickest and easiest possible way. But before we begin to discuss the actual process of training we must first understand the fundamentals that are the basis of all successful training. In other words, you must understand the *"why"* before the *"how"* so that you will know the reason for the action you perform in order to get a specific result.

There are many degrees of canine training, but first and foremost is fundamental or basic training. After basic training comes companion dog training for competition; advanced obedience training which includes trailing and scent discrimination; and there is man, or attack work, this latter training a fundamental part of the basic education given to many imported dogs, especially German Shepherd dogs which have been imported from the Fatherland where it is called Schutz Hund or "Protection Dog" training. There are also the very special educational aspects involved in gun dog, sheepherding, cattle driving, police, war dog, sled dog, performing dog, rescue dog, draught dog, commercial guard dog and blind-guide dog training. I mention these latter aspects of dog education merely to indicate how very far specialized training can go. In this book we will be mainly concerned with fundamental or basic training and our objective will be to make your dog a better canine citizen whose behavior will be impeccable in your home, your car, on the street, and when visiting.

THE KEY TO TRAINING

The key to all canine training, simple or advanced, is *control*, and control is gained, by the master over the dog, through the conditioning of the animal's reflexes, which means the molding of the shape of the dog's responses to outside stimuli. For example, if you call your hungry puppy to you with a *"beep, beep"* sound each time you feed him you will be conditioning him to come to you for the reward of food and he will associate this reward with the sound. Later the food can be eliminated but the puppy's reaction to the *"beep, beep"* sound will still be triggered by his conditioned reflexes and he will come running with the same enthusiasm as previously when the food reward was forthcoming.

Once you have gained this control over your dog you can, if you so desire, progress through basic training to advanced or specialized training in any field. The dog's only boundaries to learning, under the proper training regime, are his own limitations mentally, physically or genetically, for no single individual of any breed is fitted inherently to cope with all the active branches of specialized training. Of course not many owners possess the qualifications or experience necessary to train their dog for highly specialized tasks. But every dog owner can give, indeed it is their *duty* to give, the dog they own the necessary training to insure their pet's good conduct and gentlemanly deportment. A dog that is uncontrolled can become a nusiance

The puppy can be conditioned to obey the "Come" command at an early age through the agency of the food pan.

and even a menace that can bring grief and misery to its owner and tragedy to itself or others.

Consistency and *firmness* are the brothers to *control* and, with this trio of virtues, control, consistency and firmness, established in your own being, you are sure of success in training. Be firm, be consistent, and insist that the puppy obey once he knows what it is you want of him. Never allow him to perform an act contrary to your wish.

Other important elements of training are; keep training periods short, ten minutes at the beginning of training and lengthen the time as you proceed, but never beyond the time when your pup or dog becomes restless and loses interest; use sharp, short, distinctive words of command and always preface every command with the dog's name to capture his immediate interest; approach the training period seriously and try to schedule it at a specific time each day when there will be no outside interruptions; censure your pup when he doesn't obey; praise and reward your dog when he obeys promptly.

I am not a disciple of drastic disciplinary measures. If your dog loves you, is fairly sensitive and has a modicum of canine intelligence, he can be trained by any owner who follows the directions and sug-

Assess your pupil critically. Some dogs are more capable of learning than others, and all dogs are generally limited in training by their breed heritage.

Teaching the young puppy to stand to be groomed will pay dividends later when training the more mature animal to stand for examination.

gestions in this book. If your dog does not possess the attributes mentioned, if he either doesn't like you or doesn't care, if he is a canine moron, and if he is completely unresponsive, a clod of no sensitivity, then I suggest you either get rid of him and acquire a new dog (and this answer to the problem I highly recommend), or return this book and get your money back, because attempting to train such an animal would require the patience and insight of a saint, and I am not referring to the Bernard breed.

Direct physical punishment should only be used for one canine act . . . if your dog willfully and maliciously bites. He should be immediately and drastically punished and made to understand that this act he has committed is not to be tolerated now or ever. Physical punishment as a general form of chastisement should be avoided. Your dog loves you and wants to please you and is sensitive enough to your moods to know by the sound of your voice when you are displeased. Scold him vocally when he does wrong and praise and reward him when he pleases you. The use of rolled newspaper (which doesn't hurt, most sponsors say, just frightens through the sound it makes),

The leash is for training, not punishment, so use it for the purpose for which it was conceived. The choke collar, despite its name, is not an instrument of torture. It is the best of all training collars.

brooms, switches, your hand, the leash, or any other implement you can think of, to strike with as a form of punishment can later react unfavorably. If you strike your dog with your hand you can make him hand shy; the rolled newspaper can become the basis for his eventual chasing of the paper boy; he will learn to run and hide when your wife sweeps or vacuums the floor if you use a broom to strike him with; and the leash will become something to shrink from.

THE TEACHER

Now let us examine our teacher and pupil and see if a few valid remarks will aid in the training program about to be launched. You, the teacher or trainer, love the dog and are therefore inclined to be lenient. If you are, you will never get the required results from your training. Make your dog perform each exercise with complete consistency every time. To get this result you must yourself be consistent. You must perform each movement used in schooling, pronounce each word of command or communication in the same manner every time. For instance, do not call your dog to you with

13

the command, *"Brucie, come!"* during one training session and, in the next, call *"Brucie, here!"*, and expect the animal to understand and perform the act with alacrity and certainty. Inconsistency confuses the dog.

The most important factor of all is, as I previously mentioned, control. But, to gain complete control over your dog you must first have absolute control over *yourself*. During training if you lose your temper you lose control. Shouting, nagging repetition, angry reprimand, anger that spills over into physical chastisement, and exasperation that you make evident, all confuse your canine pupil. If he does not obey then the lesson has not been completely learned or he has become frightened by your behavior. He needs teaching, not punishment. And you, on the other hand, need to take stock of, and establish control over, your own vagaries of temperament. Training time should be a serious yet pleasant time of easy intimacy between you and your dog, a time in which a *rapport* is established between you that will heighten understanding and make your companionship more of a delight than ever before.

THE PUPIL

Let us now assess the prospective pupil's intelligence, character, and canine characteristics. His eyesight is not as keen as ours but he is quick to notice movement. Sound and scent are his chief means of communication with his world, and in these departments he is far superior to us. We must reach him, then, through voice and gesture and realize that he is very sensitive to quality change and intonation in the commanding voice. Therefore, any given command must have a definite tonal value in keeping with its purpose. The word *"No!"* used in reprimand must be expressed sharply with overtones of displeasure, while *"Good boy!"* employed as praise, should be spoken lightly and pleasantly. Words, as such, have no meaning to the dog, only the sounds they convey register in the canine mentality.

All words of positive command should be spoken sharply and distinctly, in a special "training voice" that you must develop for this specific task. Preface each command with the dog's name. The first word a puppy learns is the word-sound of his name; therefore, by using his name you immediately catch his attention and he is ready to hear and obey the command which follows. Thus, when we want our dog to come to us and his name is Boots, we command, *"Boots, Come!"*

Learn to control yourself if you wish to successfully control your dog. The act of training should be one of easy intimacy as well as serious communication. If handled correctly training will establish a delightful **rapport** between you and your dog.

Referring again to our canine pupil, we must realize that intelligence varies in dogs as it does in humans. The ability to learn and to perform is limited by intelligence, facets of character and structure, such as willingness, energy, sensitivity, aggressiveness, basic stability and functional ability. By all this I mean that the sensitive dog must be handled with greater care and quietness in training than the less sensitive animal. Aggressive dogs must be trained with great firmness; and an animal which possesses a physical fault which makes certain aspects of training painful, cannot be expected to willingly perform such tasks. As an example of this last named facet of training we can use the experience of one trainer who had a particular dog of great willingness and easy trainability who nevertheless consistently balked at the high jump. The trainer was puzzled by this strange behavior and could find no reason for it, until one day when he had occasion to take some movie film of his dogs working. When the footage arrived before the lens that showed this specific animal reluctantly performing over the high jump he slowed the film down . . . and found the answer to his problem. The dog's shoulders were not properly angulated so that when it landed, after taking the high jump, the shoulder assembly did not have enough spring and the animal consistently hit its chin painfully upon the ground before it could recover balance.

TRAINING LIMITS

There are certain limits beyond which your dog cannot go in his

Most breeds were fashioned for specific tasks and to attempt to tr

training; or perhaps I should say, beyond which it is ridiculous to attempt to push him. These boundaries are established by his genetically inherited behavior patterns. For instance it is easy to teach an English Setter to point game. It is what he has been bred for and behind this basic urge to point there are the unnumbered generations of English Setters selected for this trait, back to the time when hunters first saw certain Spaniels pause and point the hidden covey of birds before they were flushed. Man selected for this trait and the pointing breeds gradually evolved. In most of the breeds you will find a similar geneology; the selection by man for particular traits that fashioned the breed toward a specific use or purpose. It would not be feasible, therefore, to attempt to train a Pug Dog, let us say, or a German Shepherd, to point birds in the field or to do any of the work of a Gun Dog. The Pug Dog is a pet that is not physically fit for field work. The German Shepherd is a sheepherding and guard dog (among other tasks he is capable of performing), but has not inherited the desire to point game in the field. If you wish to train a dog to point, select a specimen of one of the many fine pointing breeds. If you want a dog that can be trained to herd sheep, avoid the gun dogs and select from the breeds that have been bred for generations for that specific task.

OTHER TRAINING TIPS

Always attempt to end the training period on a happy note with both you and your pupil flushed with the feeling of accomplishment.

dog to perform in an area he was not bred for is to invite failure.

Never begin training immediately after feeding. Puppies that have just been well-fed are sluggish and can't keep their minds on their work. When their bellies are empty they will perform with alacrity and are especially eager for the tidbit reward.

You will find that your dog will perform one of his lessons with gusto, probably one which fits his behavior pattern, such as retrieving an object and bringing it back to hand, which should be an easy lesson to learn for an individual of the bird dog breeds. To end each schooling period with a sense of pleasant achievement will help both of you to approach the next training session with eagerness.

Both punishment and praise must be administered *immediately* after the dog has performed the act which merits such attention. A dog's, and particularly a puppy's, memory is limited and a very short time after he has engaged in a punishable act he has forgotten all about it. It is best, especially when it is necessary to chastise the animal, to catch him while he is performing the deed and mete out his punishment at once.

Never begin a training period immediately after your dog has been fed. He will be sluggish and not as responsive as you want him to be. When his stomach is empty he is more eager to please, much more lively, and especially eager for the tidbit which you can use as a reward. This tidbit can be any kind of food that your dog particularly craves; a tiny bit of hamburger, cooked liver, peanut, kibbled biscuit, or any of the commercial tidbits. This adjunct to training should be used when teaching your puppy, but when the dog is older and has advanced in his training, the finest reward you can give him is your praise, through your voice and your caressing hand.

It is best for only one person to train a particular dog. Two or more people working the same dog leads to confusion for the animal and a subsequent lack of sureness in his performance.

Approach the dog's training with the assumption that your pupil is intelligent and, if he doesn't seem to be able to understand any of the lessons you are attempting to teach him, it is because you are not using the correct method of teaching and it is therefore *your* fault, not his. In your mind establish the idea that the opposite of *"praise"* is not *"punishment"* or *"chastisement."* Instead, think of the counter word as *"correction"*. In other words, you praise your dog for performing correctly, and you correct (*not punish*) him when he errs.

Short of a tome on the psychology of the dog or a study on canine behavior patterns, this that you have read is about all you'll need to know as a preliminary to training. Other than determination, patience, and the correct approach to the problem, which I hope you now understand, you will need a soft leather collar, a light chain choke collar and a long training leash. These will suffice for the moment as your tools of training.

Determination is a major factor in training, especially if your pupil is young, for with a sad, liquid brown eye a ten pound puppy can make a sentimental idiot of a tough, rough, two-hundred pound stevedore. Remember this fact about the wily little rascal when you begin his training.

Puppies are like children. Neither can reason so they must be taught wrong from right. If common sense is applied to initial puppy problems they can be solved with a minimum of trouble.

CHAPTER 2

EARLY TRAINING

Training begins the instant the puppies in the nest feel the touch of the breeder's hand and hear the sound of his voice. When they are being weaned the breeder generally calls them with either a wordless sound of some kind or by saying *"Come, puppies!"* when he summons them to the food which he has brought them. The puppy associates the presence of the human and the sound he makes with a pleasure-able experience and comes galloping up immediately when he hears or sees the human. His training has, in this way, begun.

Some breeders put soft collars, with small pieces of rope attached, on the puppies when they are still in the nest. In the course of their daily play the pups grab the small cords and tug and are thus more prepared for later leash breaking.

After you acquire your puppy or dog, handle him frequently and teach him to stand up at arm's length without moving. This is easy to do simply by holding him up and praising and patting him when he stands correctly, using the word *"Stand!"* as you caress him. It prepares him for easy grooming or showing, if he is that good a specimen, or for the *"Stand!"* position in his later training. Teaching the pup to stand, to come when called, and leash breaking him simply prepare him for the general training of the future. In this very early training we try to gently mold the puppy to our will and establish a friendly association which will lead naturally and easily into the more rigid training to come.

"NO", "SHAME", AND "COME"

Our first training chore is to teach the puppy to come when called. To do this we must first make the pup familiar with the name we have selected for him. At every opportunity, when playing with the pup or even when you just stop to momentarily pet him, address him by name. When you are ready to feed him or when you give him a tidbit between meals, always have him come to you, if it is only a step, and call *"Jerry, Come!"* Within a very short space of time any normal dog will answer to his name and come when called, for he associates a reward with the sound of his name and the sound of the word that summons him to you.

"No!" and *"Shame!"* are associated words that must be learned early. They must be spoken in an admonishing tone and in such a way that the youngster knows that whatever he has done to call forth these words is wrong and must not be done again.

"No!" should be used when the pup is discovered chewing on something he shouldn't be chewing on, such as the rug, furniture, or your best pair of shoes. There is a reason for his chewing, of course. He is teething and it eases the pain in his gums. Also he instinctively knows that to remove loose teeth that must come out to make way for new ones, he must chew on something. How do you handle this training problem? Simply by the application of a bit of common sense. Supply the pup with something to chew upon, either a large knuckle bone or one of the many commercial chewables manufactured for just this purpose (such as Nylabone, rawhide bone, etc.), and by using the *"No!"* command bolstered by the praising, *"Good boy!"*, delivered in the proper tone of voice, teach the pup what he can, and what he can't chew upon to ease his aching gums.

Often the pup, who is young and playful, first begins to play with shoes and curtains and various other items of the household, before he realizes it's fun to bite them, too. To avoid this unpleasantness supply the youngster with toys of his own to play with. A little common sense brought to these early, simple dog problems can save expense and aggravation. In terms of training, think of the puppy in the same way you would think of a child who is too young to reason.

The word *"Shame!"* used in training is generally associated with housebreaking but can also be used in training the pup not to chew household articles. This command must be uttered with withering disgust.

"No!" will be used throughout the animal's training or, as a

If you supply the young, teething puppy with chewables of his own he will probably ease his aching gums on these toys rather than on your household goods.

matter of fact, throughout his life, to make him aware, when it is uttered, that he has done, or is about to do, something wrong.

HOUSEBREAKING

This is usually the tragedy of the novice dog owner. But with a little knowledge and some patience it need not be as terrible a chore as it is assumed to be. First, let us find out where and when a puppy generally defecates and we will be forearmed with pertinent knowledge.

Dogs tend to defecate in areas which they, or other dogs, have previously soiled and they will go to these spots if given the chance. A puppy almost inevitably must relieve himself directly after drinking or awakening from sleep and within half an hour after eating. Avert disaster by taking him to the place you want him to use immediately. If you are breaking him to go outside, and after you have taken him out he comes in and soils the floor or rugs, he must be made to realize that he has done wrong. Scold him with, "*Shame!*" repeated several times and rush him outside again. Praise him extravagently when he has taken advantage of the great outdoors. If you catch him preparing to void in the house, a quick, sharp, "*No!*"

will often stop the proceedings and allow you time to usher him outside. Never rub his nose in his excretia as punishment. *"No!"* or *"Shame!"* appropriately delivered in an admonishing tone is punishment enough.

PAPER BREAKING

If the puppy you have bought was whelped and weaned in a paper nest then paper-breaking him will be an easy chore. Whatever material he had under his feet in the nest before you brought him home will have a good deal to do with the rapidity with which he is housebroken. He has been conditioned, and will prefer therefore, to excrete on the same kind of material he has felt underfoot and used for this purpose since he was born.

The paper should be placed in a specific area and not moved from there, the best place being a corner of the bathroom, though many people prefer a far corner of the kitchen instead. Watch the puppy for the telltale signs indicating that he is about to relieve himself and, when he begins to squat, take him to the paper immediately and

Housebreaking the puppy is the first and most arduous of all training chores. This Collie puppy is being paper broken in the house. Later he will be taught to perform outside.

The attempts at paper-breaking a puppy will never be successful if force is used at any time. A puppy will not respond in the desired manner if he is dragged to the paper and roughly restrained there.

keep him there until he goes. Then praise him highly and tell him what a fine fellow he is. Be consistent, never allow him to go any other place in the house without scolding him and taking him to the paper to show him where he *should* have gone. Sooner than you think (*you hope*) the puppy will be conditioned to run to the place you want him to when nature calls, and use the paper you have supplied for him.

Incidently, it is best, when you purchase a puppy, to bring him to his new home on a weekend. Allocate this whole weekend to making the new arrival feel at home and to the job of housebreaking. If you watch him for all the waking hours and catch him each time he has to go, show him where you want him to relieve himself and train him to go there, though it will be a tedious weekend, it will nevertheless pay big dividends in cutting down the time necessary to housebreak the pup by many hours or even days. Some older puppies can be almost completely housebroken in one weekend of concentrated training.

BOX BREAKING

If you prefer to train your puppy to evacuate in a box, the material you use in the box is important. If the tyke was born and weaned on sawdust or shavings in the whelping box, supply him with these materials in the shallow box in which you want him to relieve himself. Whatever the material he has experienced underfoot before he came to you should be used in the box. Show him what you want of him in relation to the box just as in paper breaking and he will soon be using the box all the time.

OUTDOORS BREAKING

Puppies that have been raised on earth-surfaced runs are the most easily housebroken. Simply take them out to the backyard when they are ready and, feeling familiar texture underfoot, they will readily oblige. Other than those who own Toys or very small dogs, the object of most owners is to eventually train their dog to go outside to relieve himself, even though you begin by paper or box breaking your pup. With the latter pups there must be a transition from inside to outside. To accomplish this the paper or box, previously soiled by the pup, must be moved outside and the puppy brought to it when you figure it is time for him to void. The pup, through his scenting ability, knows what the paper or box has been used for and you will usually have no trouble in urging him to utilize it again for the same purpose.

To reach the point where the puppy no longer needs the paper or box and will use the ground instead, requires a little time. The paper should be gradually decreased in size until nothing of it remains. The material in the box, after the first few days, should be removed and allowed to be used by the pup without the box. As time passes you must remove a portion of the material each day until only the earth or grass remains. When this long-looked-for time comes your puppy should be fully housebroken. Congratulations!

Incidently, when you bring the paper from the house to the yard you will probably have to anchor it with stones on each corner or you will awaken some morning to find your housebreaking bait has blown away.

I have stressed using the same material underfoot when housebreaking as the puppy is used to. There is one method of raising puppies that can cause the new owner trouble under certain circumstances, I refer to the use of raised, wire-bottom pens. The idea behind this type of kenneling is to keep puppies from reinfesting themselves with worms or coccidiosis by allowing the stools to drop through the wire to the ground below. But, since the puppy is accustomed to wire under his feet when he heeds the call of nature, he will seek a similar surface in your home. Therefore, if you have central heating or hot air heat with the grates in the floor, either don't buy that particular pup or change your home before you do buy him.

You can avoid a lot of grief by remembering a few simple rules. Until he is thoroughly clean in the house confine your pup to a particular room at night and when you leave him alone in the house. Preferably, that room should be one with a tile or linoleum floor that can be easily cleaned. Tie him so that he cannot get beyond the radius of his bed. Few dogs will soil their beds or defecate close to

After the dog has been taught to use the paper inside the house, the paper is brought outdoors. Dogs as big as this several-months-old Weimaraner are usually conditioned to relieve themselves outside.

their sleeping quarters. If the pup is still being paper or box broken in the house, whichever of these items he is using should also be within reach.

Feed at regular hours and you will soon learn the interval between the meal and its natural results and get the pup to his toilet area in time.

Give water only after meals until he is housebroken. Puppies are inveterate and constant drinkers if water is easily available, and there is no other way for water go but out. The result is odd puddles at odd times.

A trick that can be used to accelerate the pup's housebreaking is the utilization of baby suppositories. Injection of the suppository in the puppy's anus will cause a quick reaction just as it would in a child. The pup brought to the place you wish him to void will do so almost immediately if he has eaten recently and then been treated with the suppository.

Face the problem of housebreaking with aplomb, not with grimness. Laugh off the puddles, piddles and phews and, if you are thorough and determined, with a little cooperation from your pup, you will soon have a thoroughly housebroken dog and a clean house again.

Gentle, short tugs on the leash will urge the young pup to "Come." Both your voice and your hands cooperate to bring the pup to you.

Do not drag on the leash with a steady pull when you issue the "Come" command to your puppy. He will fight the leash and hang back.

COLLAR AND LEASH TRAINING

I earlier mentioned the wise breeder who adorned his pups with soft collars to which had been tied small pieces of cord. Most puppies, though, have never worn a collar or known the feeling of a leash. Purchase a narrow, soft but inexpensive collar and allow the pup to wear it constantly so he will become used to it. I recommend a cheap collar because he will soon outgrow it and you will want something better as a neck adornment for him later on. After he has worn it for two or three days attach a heavy piece of cord to it, about long enough to reach the ground. After dragging this cord around and tripping over it a time or two, the puppy will be partially leash broken, to the extent anyway that when you snap on the real leash and begin to lead him around he will not fight it if you are gentle.

Never pull a dog around on his leash. And never give the leash to a child and allow the child to pull the dog or pup around. After the leash has been attached to the collar call the puppy's name to get his attention and try to get him to come to you and walk with you of his

29

If the dog, when loose, refuses to obey the command to "Come," do not chase him. Instead, call his name and, when he turns to you, run away in the opposite direction, calling him to "Come" in a playful voice.

own accord. Play out the leash to its full length, then squat down, call the pup by name, urge him to *"Come!"* and, if he should refuse, augment the command by gentle jerks on the leash to bring him to you. Never use a long pull on the leash for any training. Instead always employ quick, short jerks. A tasty tidbit can be used to reward his obedience.

When you have the pup coming to you from the length of the leash, get a much longer, light rope, 15 to 20 feet long, attach it to his collar and repeat the same exercises you used with the leash.

If your pup is running free and you call to him to *"Come!"* but he doesn't heed your command, do *not* chase him—he will only run away and dodge your attempts to catch him and you will lose control, over yourself as well as over the pup, and many hours of training will have been wasted. Be calm, attract his attention by calling his name and, when he looks in your direction, turn and run *away* from him,

After the training workout offer the pupil a light meal. He will associate the offering of food with the end of the training session and look upon it as a reward.

looking back meanwhile and calling him to come. In most instances he will quickly run after you. Don't grab him when he reaches you. Instead squat or sit down on the ground and laugh and pet him when he comes up. Even if it takes a great deal of time and much exasperation to get him to come to you, never scold him once he has, praise him instead. If you scold him he will not know that his punishment is for *not coming*. He will associate the act of punishment with his immediate deed and will think that he is being punished for *coming* to you.

In the early stages of leash training with young puppies, be content with merely teaching the pup to move freely on the leash with only occasionally tangling it around your legs. When he is walking easily next to you you can begin using the command, *"Heel!"* to familiarize him with it. But don't attempt to make the pup rigidly *"Heel!"* until he is older. More comprehensive lessons in teaching to *"Heel!"* will be presented in a later chapter.

FEEDING AS PART OF TRAINING

Food plays a great part in your dog's training. We have seen how very early feeding makes him familiar with his call name and teaches him that there is a reward awaiting him when he comes to your call. The tidbit utilized in training as a reward is also a part of the overall feeding of the puppy to exact obedience. Training the dog to accept loud noises so that he will not be gun or thunder shy can also be accomplished during the feeding period. Trainers of hunting dogs begin teaching their future hopefulls to disregard gunshot sound during the time they are being fed. Hungry puppies are so intensely absorbed in the process of gulping down as much food as possible in as little time as possible, particularly when fed together with their litter mates, that they are prone to disregard anything, including noise, that will turn them from their purpose. The hunting dog breeder or trainer takes advantage of this absorption of the puppy in his competitive feeding by discharging a gun a short distance from where the pups are eating. The report is probably not even noticed by the food-frantic pups but is absorbed by their subconscious minds. The trainer gradually moves closer during subsequent feeding times until he can stand immediately above the youngsters and discharge the gun without disturbing them. They have been conditioned to the sound and know, by the time they become completely aware of it, that it holds no terrors for them.

It is very much worthwhile to train all puppies to be unafraid of sharp sounds and loud noises. You need not use a gun to accomplish this design. Simply take the top of a large metal can, such as a garbage can, and, when the pups are completely absorbed in their food, drop it on the floor at a short distance from where they are feeding. Gradually move closer until you can drop the top immediately behind the pups without the racket bothering them in the least. If one or two of the pups stop eating and are disturbed by the sound, soothe them and make less noise until you see that they have built up a tolerance to the sound. Storms, thunder, backfiring from autos, gunfire and sudden loud noises will find dogs trained to accept noises during feeding periods steady and fearless.

Even your own periods of feeding, the human mealtime, can be used to advantage in helping to train your dog. Do not, *ever*, feed your dog tidbits from the table while you are eating, or he will

Dogs can be trained to disregard loud noises while in the nest. Sharp and loud sounds are deliberately made while the young whelps are greedily eating a meal. Later, when mature, they will not be sound-shy. This is a method developed by breeders of gun dogs so that their stock will not be gun-shy.

There are many dog training classes throughout the country and, when you reach this
stage of advanced training, you may wish
to enjoy the stimulation that is engendered
through working with other enthusiasts in
class training.

become a mealtime pest, continually begging for food and drooling unbecomingly at the thought of attaining his desire.

Select a specific spot or area for your dog during your mealtime, and make him lie down and stay there while you eat without pestering you or anyone else at the table. A corner of the dining room is a desirable place from him to lie and wait until you are finished. Some owners banish their pets from the dining room completely while they eat. The choice, of course, is yours.

The basis of all this early training is the desire to fit your puppy into your household and make him a well behaved member of the family. The basis of all training, with dogs as it is with children, is to make them better citizens when they reach maturity by conditioning them to learning patterns of behavior and, through teaching, to acquire knowledge. With this early training as a foundation, your puppy can go on to more complicated training and you, as his owner, are the proper person to give him that training.

Many dog owners are afraid to attempt anything that smacks of advanced training. If you have successfully taught your puppy the elements of early training, including that bugaboo of the neophyte owner, housebreaking, then an attitude of apprehension toward future training is ridiculous. You have already established control and have conditioned your puppy to learn and obey your commands. The most difficult, basic part is over. Future training will be but building on the foundation you have already laid. Later, when you are engaged in advanced training, you will proably want to join a training group, one of which you will find operating in, or close to, your neighborhood. To work in the company of other people and other dogs will prove stimulating for both you and your pupil. But remember that the basis of this schooling is exactly the same as you will learn from this book—to teach you to train your dog.

Keep calm, don't shout commands, or your puppy may eventually come to think that they are reprimands. Use your voice to create word sounds that have meaning to your puppy, and never lose control of yourself for, if you do, you will lose the control you must have over your pupil, that control which is the most important part of training, the control that is the element you must use to condition your dog in the behavior patterns that will make him a well trained, well liked and admired canine citizen.

Basically the dog must be trained to gentlemanly conduct and conditioned to obey commands promptly and without hesitation. But sometimes, when the dog is young and not yet fully trained, tricks rather than direct and positive training can be utilized to advantage by the animal's owner. Keeping away from the table and the food it holds can be taught the dog through trickery.

CHAPTER 3

TRICKS OF TRAINING

There generally comes a time in the training of your young puppy, or even the older dog, when a method can be utilized that tricks the animal into the wanted behavior. This type of training is called the *negative* approach and is exactly opposite to the more widely and generally used *positive* approach. It is, in the truest sense, a form of trickery and, being disassociated from *positive* training, is also divorced from the basic control so necessary in all direct training.

These tricks are used when positive methods have failed and you feel that any drastic punishment for the pupil's failure might harm, rather than help, your training program. The basic idea behind this training trickery is to make the dog think that he is punishing himself, so the result of his disobedience must become an unforgettable experience. In the pup's mind you, his master and trainer, will have had no association with the catastrophe.

STEALING FOOD FROM TABLE

This is an act most puppies can't resist. Their exploding rate of growth pushing them to almost constant hunger, human food on the table is a delicacy they can't fight. This is particularly true of dogs that have been fed small tidbits from the table by some member of the family, one of the easiest ways to spoil a dog. Most puppies who have been scolded harshly for stealing from the table are smart enough not to attempt their crime until you are out of the room and the coast is clear. Then they will quickly and quietly sneak up to the table, delicately reach for and gobble down any food within reach, especially meat.

If your puppy, or dog, has become an inveterate thief and no amount of scolding can keep him from his shamefaced robbery when the opportunity offers, then you must turn to the negative or tricky way of correcting this misdemeanor. Arrange the table as you always do when he attempts to steal from it. Then take a tempting piece of meat, tie a string to it and to the other end of the string attach some tin cans (*empty*), bells, and whatever else you can think of that will make a racket when disturbed. Now place the piece of meat on the edge of the table. Do *not* allow the dog to watch you while you prepare his surprise. You must in no way be implicated in what is about to happen.

When all is ready leave the room as you have on previous occasions when the pup has ravished the table during your absense. When you are out of the room and the puppy stealthily approaches the table and grabs the meat, he will inadvertently pull the assortment of noise-makers attached to the other end of the string down from the table and, if he attempts to run from this frightening cacophony, it will follow him as long as he retains the stolen piece of meat in his mouth. The shock this will cause him is about the same as a sneak thief would feel who has stealthily and silently entered a home to steal and, upon opening the bureau drawer, is suddenly assailed by the earsplitting din of a brass band's close-up rendition of a Sousa march.

Careful, intense silence is the sneak-thief's cover, and once that quiet is shattered he is left naked and exposed. The sneak-thief puppy feels this same way with the din that he has caused echoing in his ears and pointing him out as the culprit. One, or at the most, two doses of this tinny pandemonium is a sure cure for puppy's table snatching.

JUMPING ON FURNITURE

The same kind of approach is used for the pup who persists, even in the face of punishment, upon jumping up and sleeping on the living room furniture. After repeated punishment he will generally only do this when you are out of the room, or the house, and will jump down as soon as he hears you returning. Telltale hair on the cushions of sofa or easy-chair is the only clue to his disobedience. To break the sly tyke of this habit we again use the negative approach and resort to trickery to make him think that he is punishing himself and that you have had nothing to do with it at all. Purchase several small mouse traps, set them and deposit them on the sofa or chair which the pup seems to favor. Then gently cover the traps with a piece of brown wrapping paper or several sheets of newspaper. Leave the room and await developments. Again let me caution you to set your trap in secret so that the victim is completely unaware that you have had a hand in his eventual consternation.

If you are close by when the pup nonchalantly leaps up to take his ease on your furniture you will hear the snapping of the smothered traps and the frantic yelp of the pup followed by his immediate departure from the vicinity. The dog can't be hurt, only startled and completely disconcerted by the snapping of the traps and the movement that accompanies this phenomena under the protective paper.

If your pup or dog is an unwelcome occupier of your bed when you aren't looking, and scolding has had no effect, the identical method used above will have the same curative result. Of course one way of avoiding all difficulty of this sort is to confine your dog to a specific area when you leave the house or are out of the room or

Don't scold your dog for jumping up on the furniture one time and the next time allow him freedom of the couch or living room chair. Be consistent in training but, if he is still too young to mind well, he can be tricked into keeping off the furniture.

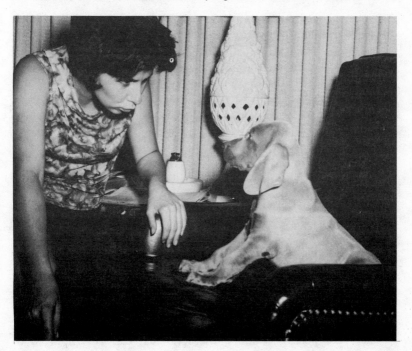

The master's bed is soft and comfortable and, if scolding doesn't make the culprit stay off the bed, then a little trickery should be resorted to.

occupied elsewhere. This area would not allow him to be near bedroom or living room and so temptation would be removed. But to my mind it is better to allow the dog, assuming he is fully housebroken, the run of the house and to face and correct any training problems that follow in the wake of this freedom.

JUMPING UP ON PEOPLE

Dogs of boisterous temperament have a tendency to constantly jump up on their master, mistress, the people of the household and all visiting friends. In this way they exhibit their joy of life and love of you. But this happy greeting can be the means of your losing innumerable and valuable friends when your mud-footed dog jumps up on some natty visitor who is wearing a new suit or dress. Such behavior under such circumstances can even exasperate you, the animal's loving owner.

There are positive training methods that can be employed to

Dogs that jump up on people can become very unpopular, especially in muddy or rainy weather. A training trick can make them heartily sick of ever jumping up on anyone again.

break this habit that will be explained later. But now I will explain another trick to use if the "*No!*" command alone does not break him of this habit. When he jumps up grinning and pawing, grab his front feet and retain your hold, meanwhile greeting him with good-humored tolerance. The pup finds himself in an uncomfortable position standing on his hind legs alone, a position not quite suitable or natural for one of the canine species. He will soon tire of standing in such a way and begin to pull and tug to release his front paws from your hands and return to a normal position with all four paws on terra firma. Retain your hold in the face of his gradually more frantic struggles until he has become heartily sick of his position and the whole idea. A few such lessons and he will refrain from committing an act that brings such discomfort in its wake.

If the dog is a large one you can add to his discomfort by reaching forward with your toe and stepping on his hind foot as you hold his front paws. Be careful not to step too hard. Your object is to cause the animal discomfort, not to break or bruise his toes.

You will probably be able to think of other little tricks that you can improvise to outsmart your dog in some area of conduct. But remember that these tricks are only short-cut ways of rectifying nuisance habits, and do nothing to establish the control and "*rapport*" which must exist between trainer and dog in the important area of positive training.

MORE TRICKS OF TRAINING

I have seen trainers use a strange mode of punishment which seems to have worked with some puppies. A rolled up piece of paper is used, preferably brown wrapping paper, not newspaper. When the puppy chews upon a forbidden object, his master's shoe let us say, the trainer, with the puppy kept close so that he will not miss what happens, uses the rolled paper to strike and punish the *shoe*, not the puppy. Some pups react by never again touching the punished object or any others like it. But I have also seen the opposite occur and have had puppies attack and attempt to aid their master in his punishment of the naughty object.

It is essential that puppies as well as grown dogs be given their freedom and allowed to run off leash often. Many dogs, kept confined to the leash, act like wild idiots when set free. Sometimes such animals run so far and fast that they are quickly out of sight and seem

The dog running loose off leash can be easily trained not to get too far ahead of his owner or trainer by conditioning him to constantly check back to see if you are in plain sight.

deaf to the frantic calls of their owners. One way to cure this habit is, of course, to give them more freedom. But there is a way to condition your dog to stay closer to you when walking or running off leash. This, too, is a trick, but one that is fun for both you and your dog. Simply hide when he begins to get too far away, then call or whistle him to you. Upon looking back he won't see you and will come searching until he finds you. If he seems to be unable to find you give your position away by some movement or slight noise. It is a game he will enjoy, but in the playing of it he will learn to constantly look back to make sure you are in sight and he will always stay fairly close so that he can return immediately to enjoy your game of hide-and-go-seek.

By holding a tidbit high over your dog's head so that he must strain to peer up at it, and inadvertently sits to be more comfortable, is a method sometimes employed by trainers to make a dog sit. The

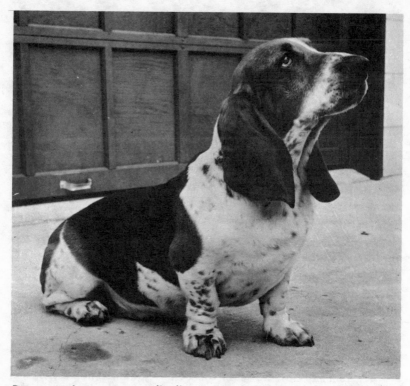

Dogs can be trained to "Sit" by negative methods or through the employment of a tidbit, coupled with the command "Sit" to condition the dog to obey.

word "*Sit!*" is spoken when the dog lowers his hindquarters to the ground for comfort.

Dog psychologists have long used negative methods of conditioning animal reflexes to get specific training results. The bell and meal test is well known. Dogs, conditioned to be fed at certain hours, were alerted to the feeding time by the ringing of a bell. Eventually just the ringing of the bell would bring saliva to the dog's mouth even though food was not forthcoming.

Using small metal clickers of the type that were once commonly found in popcorn boxes in the shape of a frog is another approach psychologists have used in conditioning behavior patterns of dogs. When the dog naturally indulges in a specific action, such as turning toward a corner of the room, the psychologist clicks the little tin instrument. Soon he has conditioned the dog to turn toward that specific corner of the room every time the clicker sounds.

I have used this type of conditioning myself in training. It takes tremendous concentration, complete absorption in the task at hand, and time without interruption spent with the pupil. I taught a nine months old bitch to sit and lie down by staying with her constantly for three days. Every time she would normally sit I would utter the command, "*Sit!*" Every time she would naturally lie down I said, "*Lie down!*" I did not touch her or ever force her to obey these commands, I simply stayed with her constantly as a completely absorbed observer and each time she performed, of her own accord, either of the desired actions I gave the proper command as she executed them. She was soon conditioned to obey these commands immediately without having been forced into the proper positions by positive training. Granted it was a tedious and time-consuming task, it nevertheless proved to my own satisfaction that it could be done with gratifying results.

Remember, when you use these tricks to condition your dog to behave the way you want him to, you are not actually training him,

The same type of negative training can be used to make your dog obey the "Lie down" command. This kind of conditioning is tedious, limited in scope, and does not bring the "rapport" between trainer and dog that positive training provides.

Most dogs thoroughly enjoy riding in the family car. But they must be trained to car deportment and, when young, taught to ride without getting motion sickness.

you are only tricking him to perform certain acts that will mold his conduct, and this method of negative training is limited in scope. I could go on, telling you of other similar means of training such as those used by hunters, where a reward of meat, and punishment through electric shock, is used in negative training. Electrical devices can be constructed to fit the dog's collar and used to shock him when he disobeys in training. Electric prods, such as cattlemen use, are also utilized by some trainers. I am personally against all training methods, negative or positive, that are based on cruel punishment. Shocking or actually hurting a dog is not necessary in basic training. Such methods are the devices of sadists, or calloused individuals who should not own dogs, not dog trainers.

If you own a dog that you can't control or train, do not beat him or use cruel methods in your attempt to train him. Take him instead to a qualified dog trainer, explain your problem to him and allow him to train your dog for you. It is the business of such men to deal with problem dogs or to train dogs for specialized tasks. To them your dog will be just another pupil who has come to their canine school to learn proper conduct.

CAR TRAINING

To train your pup to ride with aplomb in the family car is merely a matter of repetition. Make the first few rides very short, increasing the distance as he gains in his ability to endure the movement of the car without upset. Always make sure that he enters the car for these lessons in riding with an empty stomach. Dogs love to accompany their masters, or any member of the family, when they go for a drive.

Of course there is another kind of car training and that is breaking your dog from chasing cars if he has acquired that nasty and dangerous habit. A heavy cord attached to his collar to which a piece of broomstick is horizontally hung, just low enough to bounce sharply against his legs if he starts running, is a negative method of training. If the ordinary *"No!"* or *"Shame!"* or the broomstick doesn't stop him from continuing this practice then a harsher method must be used. This must be accomplished with the assistance of someone in a car which we assume he will chase. The person in the car must be supplied with a water pistol filled with water, and while the car is in motion and the dog chases it barking, he must squirt the dog full in the face with the water. If this method still proves fruitless, a weak solution of ammonia should be used in the water pistol instead of plain water. This might seem like a drastic means of combating such behavior, but you must remember that the end result of car chasing is either the death of your dog under the wheels of some speeding vehicle, or the wreck of a chased car with human injury and possible loss of life as an aftermath.

The first formal, or "positive" training for both dog and pupil begins with the "Sit" position. The trainer learns how to handle leash, voice, and dog with finesse, and the dog learns the most elementary and important of training exercises.

CHAPTER 4

SERIOUS TRAINING BEGINS

What you have learned about training in this book up to now has been preliminary training for the young puppy, with the exception of a very few lessons such as car chasing, etc. Between the ages of two and six months your puppy should have absorbed all the teaching that has gone before. Now we approach the time of serious training.

If possible, it is best to arrange to conduct two training sessions a day. Begin with ten minute sessions if you can manage two a day. If you only have time for one training session, limit the time to from 15 minutes to half an hour. Observe your dog during the training period and you will be able to tell when he begins to become bored with the whole thing. That is the time to quit. As you and your pupil advance in your schooling the time limit can be extended.

The training commands you are about to teach your dog are the most important in relation to fashioning your pet into a fine and gentlemanly companion. The lessons he will learn are: to sit, to heel, to lie down, to come when called, to stand upon command, and to stay when told to, in the sit, down, and stand. He will learn a few other commands too, if you wish to teach them to him, but those mentioned here, at the beginning of this chapter, are the commands of basic schooling.

Before we begin let us be sure that we are in an area where there will be no activity that will distract the dog from concentration on his work. Reprise in your mind all that you have learned so far about control and all the other elements of training in relation to you and your dog. Check your equipment and be sure that the choke-chain collar is being correctly worn and that the leash is gathered easily in

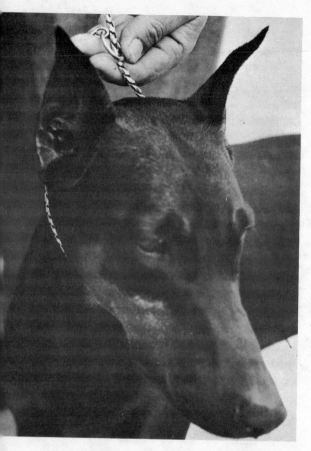

This is the proper way to apply the chain choke collar. When worn correctly it will not pinch the dog or cut the neck hair and it can be used to best advantage by the trainer.

your right hand. You will also use your left hand on the leash, but the bulk of the leash must be gathered and held in your right hand. Remember always to work your dog from your left side. And do *not* allow your pupil to consider this play. He must be taught that these periods of training are serious, are work, not play, and that following them he will be allowed to play to his heart's content.

TRAINING TO "SIT!"

You have probably given your puppy some schooling in this exercise already. But now he must be taught how to sit exactly and immediately when given the command, and to do it on leash and at your side.

Maneuver the dog to your left side and, holding the leash in your right hand to allow your left hand to be free and to give you about a foot of slack in the leash from the dog's neck to your right hand, get your dog's quick attention by speaking his name immediately followed by the command, *"Sit!"* Issue the command firmly and clearly in your best training voice. As you do, pull upward on the leash until the collar begins to tighten and, with your free left hand, reach back, and place your palm on his croup or rump, your fingers facing toward his tail. Now press downward firmly with your left hand to force his hind legs to fold and his hind end to collapse into a sitting position. While you do this be sure that you keep the leash held in your right hand fairly taut so that you hold his head and the front part of the dog up.

When your pupil is in the correct position praise him with a *"Good boy!"* or *"Good girl!"* as the case may be. Incidently, throughout this book I have assumed that the pupil is masculine. Believe me, I have nothing against the feminine gender, animal, mineral, vegetable, or what-have-you. On the contrary, under most circumstances I rather favor them. In this instance, though, I simply find it easier to use the masculine gender when referring to the pupil.

Two phases of the proper way to make a dog sit.

The wrong way to handle the leash for the "Sit." At right, the dog in the finished "Sit."

When you have your pupil sitting nicely at your side, relax the tautness of the leash as you praise him but attempt to keep him sitting. To do this you must be quiet, not boisterous in your praise. Now, with a quick, gentle tug on the leash, move forward a step to bring your dog standing and at your side. Repeat the lesson again, being careful not to tighten the leash too sharply as you reach down and push the dog's hindquarters down. Straighten your body and keep the dog sitting for a few seconds at your side before you step forward to repeat it again.

Should your dog quit sitting and stand of his own accord, then it is not necessary to step forward before repeating the command. But you must not allow him to bounce back up to his feet immediately. When you feel the dog's rump begin to yield under your hand as you press down and give the "*Sit!*" command, use less pressure to make him sit, until the mere touch of a finger on his croup gets the desired result. Soon, then, you will not have to touch him at all, just speak the command and he will sit quietly at your side.

If your dog will not hold the sit position for more than a second or two before he breaks, scold him with a "*No!*" and make him take the position again. Should he lie down when told to sit, don't attempt to pull him up by the leash, lift him from in front until he is in the "*Sit*" position. Correct his position by placing your hand on his rump either to the right or the left side when you push down, whichever side will correct his posture if he sits crookedly.

The sit is the easiest of all the exercises, which is why I recommend that it be taught first. But, being the first lesson, it must be learned perfectly. Therefore do not settle for less than perfection from your pupil. Do not tolerate any degree of sloppiness. Your dog must sit promptly and squarely at your side when given the "*Sit*" command. Though at the beginning it is permissible to use the command several times as you push down on his rump to make him obey, after he has learned what you want of him give the command just once, using his name first, "*Jerry, sit!*"

This first lesson, to properly sit, will set the tone for all the schooling to come. Both you and your dog will learn a great deal before you move on to the next lesson. It is up to you to see that your dog learns to be a perfectionist in his execution of this simple command.

In an earlier chapter I told you how I tricked a bitch into obeying the "*sit*" and "*down*" commands by speaking the proper order each time she, of her own accord, began to sit or lie down. Such negative conditioning can be indulged in when the puppy is very young, but I do not recommend that it be used in the direct and positive training that you have now begun. I was conducting an experiment with an older bitch when I used this form of approach, a very tedious experiment I might add, and not one to be used after positive-conditioning schooling has been successfully started.

The importance of the "*Sit!*" command, and its exact execution, will become obvious later. For in the training to come you will find that most of the new lessons will begin from the sit position.

Training your dog to heel is the initial phase
of teaching him gentlemanly conduct when
walking with you outdoors.

CHAPTER 5

TRAINING TO "HEEL!"

The "*sit*" position has trained your dog to sit nicely at your side where he is ready to begin to learn how to "*heel*". He need not be perfect in the "*sit*" before you begin this new lesson. As a matter of fact, while you are teaching the "*sit*" in your very first lesson, if, after the pupil is doing fairly well in obeying the "*sit*" command, you sense that he is becoming restless, it is then time to switch to the new lesson of "*heeling*".

Stand straight with the dog in a good sit position at your side. The leash should be gathered in your right hand with the left hand grasping the leash so that it hangs from the dog's collar with about two feet of slack. Your left leg should be close to the dog's shoulder, touching it if possible. Now you step briskly forward, with your left foot first, using a definite, long stride. As you do this you jerk quickly on the leash with your left hand and give the command, "*Brucie, heel!*" Speak his name a split second before you stride forward to get his quick attention, and follow it with the command and the leash tug. His name prepares him for action and your movement forward and jerk on the leash is the action with which he will couple the command.

Repeat the command "*Heel!*" (now without the animal's call name) every few steps once you get him moving. At first he will probably run ahead, drag behind, or lurch to the side. Whatever he may do can be controlled by short jerks on the leash with your left hand once you get him moving. Always be sure that there is slack in the leash, otherwise you will not be able to jerk it so that the chain choke collar tightens quickly and is released again, which is the measure of your control over the pupil.

Once you have the dog moving fairly well in the heel position in a

"Heeling" properly and well. The leash is held in a manner that gives the trainer complete control over the animal.

straight line, make a sharp right turn, alerting the animal with a tug on the leash and the command "*Heel!*" Walk straight forward again for forty or fifty steps, or to a given mark, and repeat the right turn using the same means of conveying your wants to the pupil as you did before. After you have completed a square in this manner, make a complete right about turn, speaking the "*Heel!*" command supplemented by a tug on the leash, or several tugs if necessary to get him around.

Continue a few more right-about turns with the appropriate command and leash jerks, and then come to a halt and command your pupil to, "*Mike, sit!*" If he seems confused and doesn't sit immediately, reach down with your left hand and touch or put slight pressure upon his croup to remind him of what he must do.

Combine these two commands, "*Heel*" and "*Sit*", until your dog automatically comes to a sit position at your side when you come to a halt. In other words, he will sit without command when you have him at heel and come to a complete halt.

Once he has assimilated the heeling lesson and walks nicely at your side close to your knee there is no need to keep repeating the "*Heel!*"

The wrong way to attempt to teach the pupil to "Heel." The dog is being dragged by the leash.

command unless you are about to make a turn. Now, since he no longer needs the small tugs or leash jerks for signals to keep at heel, your left hand will be free to give him a visual as well as an oral signal and command to heel. This is done by gently slapping the side of your thigh as you give the signal to "*Heel!*" Soon your dog will learn to watch for the visual "*Heel!*" signal and it will no longer be necessary for you to augment it with the oral command. On turns the slap of your hand against your leg will gain his alert attention as did your spoken "*Heel!*" before.

THE "HALT" SIGNAL

When you train the dog to "*Heel!*" you must, necessarily, come eventually to a stop. To keep your animal from continuing his forward movement when you come to a stop, you must employ the signal, "*Halt!*" A step or two before you come to a stop and utter the "*Halt!*" command, tighten up on the leash to prepare your pupil for what is to come. Soon he will know that this tightening of the leash is a signal and he will be alert to the command to "*Halt!*" If he continues walking when you stop, don't pull him back with a long, forceful pull on the leash. Use instead the short jerks, slap your thigh and call him to "*Heel!*" Continue the exercise until he knows and reacts faithfully to the command to "*Halt!*"

During the lessons in heeling, no matter what your dog does, short of throwing himself to the ground and lying on his back, you must continue walking at a steady gait. If he goes wide at the turns, bring him to you with short jerks on the leash, but do not stop your steady forward stride. When he closes up nicely on the turns, reward him with a "*Good boy!*" but don't slow down or quit your precise forward walking. Of course your pace must be matched to the size of your pupil. A brisk pace for a German Shepherd or Labrador would keep a Peke or Boston at an impossible run. Some breeds are capable of moving faster than others, so accommodate your pace to that of the breed your pupil represents.

Work your dog in the "*Sit*" and "*Heeling*" exercises for at least three training sessions, or three training days if his training is scheduled for one session daily.

When you begin teaching your dog to left turn while heeling, step to the left with your left leg, the leg closest to the dog. This almost

automatically turns him to the left. With smaller dogs you can step in front of and turn them by jerks on the leash. Mix up your turns during the lessons to keep your pupil attentive and to condition him to always be alert while heeling so that he will not miss a turn.

Often, after your dog has learned to "*Heel!*" properly and well, he will begin to move a bit ahead of you and in this way miss turns. Small dogs can usually be corrected by jerks on the leash to bring them back to the proper position. This will sometimes work with larger dogs, too. But

Match your pace to the size of your pupil. Short strides keeps this Shih Tzu moving well.

If other methods fail to keep your animal from surging ahead when "Heeling," the author demonstrates how to correct this fault through the ____ use of the whirling leash.

if it doesn't, we must try another way to keep him from surging too far forward while at heel. Allow the slack of the leash, that you have up to now held gathered in your hand, to fall loose, over your hand. The long training leash should allow three to four feet of slack to hang from your right hand, with the leash's looped handle at the end. Now begin to whirl this slack around in a circle in front of you as you move your dog forward in the "*Heel!*" position. As soon as he begins to surge too far in front the whirling end of the leash will hit his nose and he will draw back from it. Continue this treatment until the dog stays properly at your side when heeling.

This way of correction is, of course, again a trick, not positive teaching. The dog does not associate his punishment with either you or the leash. He feels that he has brought it upon himself by moving into the path of the whirling leash.

Let us suppose that your animal genius has quickly learned how to sit and heel and does both with a nice élan and flourish. It is time then to introduce you, your pupil, and your little smile of triumph to our next training exercises.

Hand signals are as important in training as
the proper use of your voice and the leash.
Eventually the pupil will unerringly obey
your hand signals even when they are not
augmented by vocal commands.

CHAPTER 6

TRAINING TO "SIT—STAY" AND "DOWN"

We have taught our dog a hand signal for heeling and it is now time to teach him to "*Stay*" while at the "*Sit*" position and introduce him to a hand signal to supplement the oral command in this exercise. We will also teach him to obey a hand signal for the "*Sit*" alone, and from a position in front of the dog.

"SIT-STAY!"

Let us begin with the "*Sit-stay!*" because after learning the "*Sit*" and "*Heel*" exercises he will be in the natural position to be taught this new lesson.

Begin with your dog in the now familiar sit position at heel on your left side. The leash is gathered as usual in your right hand. Now reach down with your free left hand with the palm flat and toward the dog and put the flat of your palm, fingers pointing toward the ground, in front of his nose speaking the command, "*Sit-stay!*" As you give the command, step out and away from the pupil with your *right* leg.

Remember that when we taught our student to heel we always led with our *left* foot forward. That was to remove the close support of that leg from beside the dog so that he knew that you were moving away and would begin to follow. This time, when teaching him the "*Sit-stay*" we want him to remain where he is so we step out first with the other, the right leg.

As you step forward pass the leash from your right to your left hand and, from your long stride away, turn to face the dog holding the leash high and rather taut to control him, repeating as you face

The beginning of the "Sit-stay." The dog is at "Sit," the trainer is using the proper hand signal (using the **left** hand as advocated by the author), and is about to step away from the pupil.

him the command, "*Sit-stay!*" Your repeat of the command and the tightening of the leash, held at arms length over the dog, is designed to keep the animal from following you.

If he stays in the sit position upon command when you stand in front of him, reverse everything you have just done and go back to his side again. Go through the whole procedure again and continue to do so until he sits firmly at the command and when you leave his side and evidently knows what you want him to do. Now you can vary the procedure by taking a step to the left, a step to the right, when you face him, and finally walk completely around him, always ending up at his side and always begining with the first step forward and the turn to face him. Keep repeating the command, "*Stay!*" to hold him in the proper position, using it as often as necessary. If he indicates that he is about to rise and come to you, utter the command sharply.

The leash now held in your left hand, to which you passed it when you stepped forward away from the dog, leaves your right hand free,

Leaving the dog in the "Sit-stay." The trainer is stepping away from the pupil with the **right** leg and is about to turn and face the animal.

and this, your right hand, should be held out toward the pupil with the palm up, fingers pointing upward, in the "*Stay!*" sign. Though the fingers pointed downward when you first gave the signal in front of the animal's nose as you stepped away from him, the flattened palm turned toward him is, to the dog, the visual signal of the "*Stay!*" command whether the fingers point up or down.

SECOND STEP OF "SIT-STAY!"

When the pupil will remain in the "*Sit-stay!*" for ten or fifteen seconds as you engage in taking your one stride away in several directions while holding the leash at arms length above him to check his movement, you may begin the second step of this exercise.

Exchange the leash for a long, thin but strong, nylon cord about thirty feet long. Incidently, this cord can be later used for the "*Come*" or "recall" exercise. Go through the same "*Sit-stay!*" routine as you did when the dog was wearing a leash instead of the rope which now replaces it. But this time do not attempt to hold the rope up and over the dog's head to restrain him as you did before. Instead allow the rope to hang loose. When the exercise is finished to your satisfaction, praise your pupil lavishly.

Again you must repeat the whole routine from the beginning. Now, as you step away don't just take one step, take two. Watch the dog closely and be ready to check any movement toward you with a sharp, "*Sit-stay!*" Move around him in a circle and widen the circle as you progress, until you have played out half the rope and can circle him at a distance of about fifteen feet. Return to him and your proper position next to him, praise him and release him. If he will "*Sit-stay!*" for a full minute while you circle him and return, he has done well.

If your dog simply will not "*Sit-stay!*" as you step forward, begin the exercise by stepping to the side away from him. This often corrects any tendency he may have to stand and follow you.

Most trainers use the palm-toward-the-dog signal for the "*Sit-*

The dog at "Sit-stay" and being held in that position by the raised and admonishing forefinger of the trainer, the hand signal recommended by the author.

stay", as I have indicated before. It is fine to use as you leave your dog's side in the "*Sit-stay!*" but it has been my experience that it is an awkward gesture once you face your dog. I, personally prefer to use a raised, rather admonishing, forefinger of the right hand as the "*Sit-stay!*" sign once I have left the dog's side and stepped in front of him.

TRAINING TO "DOWN!"

There are several ways to accomplish this exercise depending upon the individual dog, his size and temperament. If your dog is small enough, the easiest method is to begin in the usual manner with your dog at the "*Sit!*" position at your left side. With the leash gathered in your right hand, reach down with your left, leaning over the dog, and with the flat of your palm press down on his shoulders (withers) until you force him to lie down, accompanying the downward push with the vocal command, "*Prince, Down!*" Repeat the

If your pupil is too large to force into the "Down" position by pressure on the withers, do not attempt to push him down with your weight. This merely leads to an undignified and futile form of wrestling.

Jumping is good exercise for your dog. The jump must be adjusted to the size of the pupil, as it has been for these two Scotties who are about to retrieve the dumbbells in the foreground.

This Airedale has taken the dumbbell and is returning over the jump.

Remember that your praise and a demonstration of the love you bear your dog is more important to him than any tidbit.

When training your dog to **"Heel"**, adjust your pace to his. A short-legged dog attempting to keep up with a long-legged trainer may become discouraged and quit trying to obey the command.

Obeying the **"Down"** signal, both vocal and physical, can drop your dog from a distance and keep him from running out onto a road where dangerous traffic might injure or kill him.

Using the "Leash stepover" method of forcing the pupil to "Down." Through the use of simple leverage the animal is forced into the desired position. This is the first step with the dog still at "Sit."

word "*Down!*" over and over again to keep him in the down position once you have forced him into it.

If your dog is a member of one of the larger breeds, and he resists your downward push to the extent where it becomes almost impossible to accomplish your objective, then you must approach this exercise from a different angle.

Begin with the "*Sit-stay!*" and when you are facing the pupil reach forward as you give the command, grasp the dog's front legs just above the feet and pull the feet toward you. This action will cause the animal's body to drop down to the ground and he will be in the "*Down!*" position. As soon as he has inadvertently assumed this posture, put the flat of your palm on his shoulders and press downward to hold him there meanwhile repeating the command over and over again.

Should your dog be stubborn and adamant in his refusal to "*Down!*" and the above approaches have failed, then we must resort to yet another method. Begin again as you have before with the dog at "*Sit-stay!*" with you, the trainer, facing your dog. Hold the leash in your left hand with enough slack in it so that it loops a few inches above the ground. Now put your left foot over the leash so that the lowest section is under your instep. Speak the command, "*Down!*" and simultaneously pull up on the leash and press down with your foot to the ground. This action will tighten the choke chain and put a downward pressure on the dog forcing him into the desired position.

If you squat or kneel in front of the dog when he is in the down position he will probably remain there instead of jumping up immediately. Once you have made him understand what it is you want of him and he obeys, then use a hand signal. In this case the

Leverage applied, the dog has been forced into the "Down" position and the second and last step has been accomplished. The pressure applied by your foot on the leash will hold the animal in position.

Your pupil must learn to **"Sit"** properly, his position in obeying this command corrected by hand, as shown in the top picture, if necessary. On the left the German Shepherd is in a perfectly balanced **"Sit"** position next to his handler.

If you don't want your pet to use the furniture be firm and consistent (**as you must be in all training**) in ordering him off.

If you can catch your dog committing an act of which you disapprove and chastise him, he will quickly avoid repeating the act again.

The "Down-stay" is easier to teach your pupil than the "Sit-stay," because the animal is in a more relaxed position when lying down.

outstretched arm moved from overhead downward with the hand flat and palm down, is the sign for the *"Down!"*

THE "DOWN-STAY!"

Though the *"Down!"* is sometimes difficult to accomplish initially, once grasped by the dog it is easily learned in one scholastic session. The *"Down-stay!"* should not take your pupil more than one session to master either, though he will not perform it for any great length of time satisfactorily until the sixth or seventh session. In comparison, the *"Sit!"* and the *"Sit-stay!"* ordinarily take three or four sessions before the dog finds ease in obeying the commands. The reason for this difference in learning time is because in the *"Down-stay!"* the animal is in a more fitting and relaxed position to *"Stay!"*

In teaching the *"Down-stay!"* you first accomplish the *"Down!"* then add the *"Stay!"* signal as you did in the *"Sit-stay!"* Repeat until the dog obeys.

If the dog attempts to crawl toward you, to get up and come to

Keep the animal in the "Down-stay" position with hand signal and vocal command until you wish to release him.

you, or to sit up, attempt to check him at the first indication of movement. Quickly and sharply utter the command, "*Stay!*" and "*Down-stay!*"

After each lesson has been learned, go through the whole routine, repeating all the lessons that your pupil has absorbed from the beginning. End the session with a lesson he knows well so you finish on a note of accomplishment and pride, then with lavish praise engage in a little triumphant romp with your canine genius to bring the lesson to a pleasant close.

Teach your puppy to chew on toys and objects you have supplied him with specifically for that purpose, not on personal and expensive property.

Keep your dog from becoming a drooling pest during your mealtime. Teach him to stay in a particular **"place"** until you have finished.

Small puppies must be taught to walk up and down stairs. Be gentle and patient and **coax** the pup into mastering this chore.

Housebreaking need not be the terrible job most puppy owners expect. Be watchful, firm, and use reprimand and praise to the fullest extent.

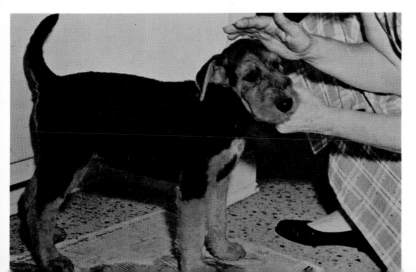

The "Recall" or "Come when called" exercise begins with the pupil at "Sit-stay" and, through the medium of voice, hands and leash, the dog is brought in to "sit" in front of the trainer.

CHAPTER 7

TRAINING TO "COME!"

In an earlier chapter I stressed the fact that you must never scold or punish your dog when he has come to you regardless of the provocation. If you have not followed this advice, or if you have forgotten it, you will pay for your negligence now in the *"Come when called"* exercise.

Exact obedience to this command is absolutely essential for it can save your dog's life and keep you from embarrassment, for there is nothing more exasperating then attempting to catch a loose dog that won't come to you. Your pupil had learned the rudiments of the *"Come!"* command, as he has several of the other directives, when he was much younger. But now it is time to condition him to obey faithfully, absolutely, and with alacrity the moment the command is uttered.

To begin this exercise (known in obedience parlance as the *"recall"*), we bring the pupil to the *"sit"* position at our side, give him the command and the hand signal to *"Sit-stay!"* and walk away in front of him to the limiting length of the loosely held leash in your right hand. Command him to *"Spot—Come!"* in a crisp voice and simultaneously jerk on the leash to direct him toward you. Guide him to a position directly in front of you with quick leash tugs and the crisply spoken command and when he has accomplished your desire pet and praise him lavishly.

Remember that you have given him a direct order, the *"Stay!"* which he is now being asked to break or disregard and, if you have succeeded in training him truly and well, it will be difficult for him to respond without reluctance. Because the pupil is loathe to disobey the *"Stay!"* command, you must do whatever you can to coax him

Alert and eagerly awaiting the next command this Shepherd symbolizes the pleasure an owner can derive from a fully trained and vigilantly obedient dog.

Children and puppies are a familiar combination and both species of youngster must be trained and conditioned to take their places in their individual worlds.

A Doberman in the proper sit position before his trainer, delivering the dumbbell to hand after the retrieve over the jump. Below, the author's Shepherds holding the long **"Sit"** upon command, resulting in a fine "family" portrait.

This dog, executing the "Come" exercise with dash and elan, is ready to begin working and learning the same lesson on the long line.

to obey the recall. Your position as you give the command will help. Kneel, squat, or lean far over toward him, positions that have a beguiling effect upon the dog, acting as a compulsion to movement toward you. Slap your knee gently as a hand signal which is also an aid in compelling him to come to you.

Do *not* give him the "*Sit*" command when he has arrived at a position directly before you. The accomplishment of the "*Come!*" is enough to warrant your unmitigated praise. If he *should* sit in front of you in completing the "*Come!*" exercise, it is an added bonus.

USE OF THE LONG LINE

Once the pupil understands the "*Come!*" command and executes it with commendable speed on leash, the next step is to train him to come from a greater distance through the use of the long rope. Remove the leash and attach the nylon (or rope) line to his collar and, starting with the "*Sit!*" position, use the line exactly as you did the leash but move further away. By looping the line to the side as you move away from the dog you will keep him from becoming

This picture is a very important reminder that praise should be given your pupil after every well-done exercise. This short period of relaxation and intimacy is good for both trainer and pupil.

If you intend entering your animal in dog show conformation competition, the **"Stand-stay"** command takes on new importance and usefulness.

Teaching the puppy to stand easily, without moving or sitting, during the process of grooming will pay later training dividends.

On leash and in the wanted **"Stand-stay"** position at the trainer's side. This Irish Setter will never soil himself by sitting in mud or water while walking with his owner during inclement weather.

entangled in it. It is best, at this stage, not to attempt to reel in the line as he comes to you since this will keep both hands employed so that you cannot give the hand signal, and it might also tend to distract the dog.

When you have your dog coming to you quickly and without hesitation when you speak the "*Spot—Come!*" command, combine it with the "*Sit!*" As he comes up, and when he is directly in front of you and *close*, give him the "*Sit*" command so that he comes in on the recall and sits in front of you.

CORRECTING FAULTS IN THE RECALL

Should your dog evince a nonchalant attitude toward the recall, if he ambles slowly toward you instead of coming in with the snap and interest he should display, then it will be necessary to reel in the rope as he comes so that you can keep it taut and aid him to a faster pace by quick, sharp tugs on the line. Meanwhile move backward, away from the dog. You may find that you will have to skip backward away from him in quick steps to make him follow with increasing alacrity.

Once a dog has broken the "*Stay!*" command, as he must to obey the recall, he may break too fast and begin to follow you as soon as you step away from him. Reproach him with "*No!*" and make him remain at the "*Stay!*" until you give him the "*Come!*" command. When you face him to give the latter command, wait a few seconds, holding him in the "*Stay!*" command, before you counteract it with the recall signal. Move a few paces to the left, then to the right before you return directly in front of him and release him from the "*Stay!*" with the new recall command.

Remember that your dog's eyesight is not comparable to his hearing or sense of smell, so when you call him in from a distance it is best not to give a hand signal. He may confuse it with a visual signal used by you for one of the other commands. Use the oral command only and, after he works properly to it, there is no reason for you to shout it. His auditory ability is much greater than any human's.

This shouting of commands as it is taught by many obedience trainers to be emulated by their human pupils who, in turn, use it upon their own animals to enforce obedience, is not at all necessary or desirable. Only at the beginning of training should the trainer's voice be fairly loud, yet even then, not a shout. Each command must be expressed distinctly and with good diction so that it can be understood by the pupil and differentiated from other commands. As the dog becomes more familiar with the commands and works quickly, surely and smoothly to obey, the trainer's voice can be appreciatively lowered until all orders are issued in an easy, but distinct, conversational tone.

COMBINING COMMANDS

By combining all the lessons your dog has learned up to this point you can now take him through a very satisfactory pattern of obedience and extract from him a performance that is a glowing tribute to your ability as a trainer and to your pupil's mental competence.

Beginning with the "*Sit!*" you move the dog off briskly in the "*Heel!*" position, executing several turns and figure eights. Finishing

Combining the "Sit" and "Come" exercises brings your pupil in for the "Finish."

Trained to **"Sit"** while on leash, the owner is moving away from the side of his charge to stand in front of him.

Fully trained in the **"Sit"**, off leash, this Collie is obeying the hand signal of his mistress to **"Sit-stay"**.

The **"Come"** command, when off leash,
must always be promptly obeyed, and
will be if earlier conditioning has been
well done.

The handler of this Boston is using the
most direct and simple technique to
teach her dog this most important
training segment, to obey the **"Sit"**
command.

the "*Heel!*" your pupil "*Sits*" again at your side. You now execute the "*Sit-stay!*" followed by the "*Down-stay!*" and, after moving around the dog to the side, back and front to illustrate his sureness in the "*Stay!*" you return to his side and call him once again to the "*Sit!*" position. From "*Stay!*" in this position you move away from him for the recall when he will return to sit in front of you.

Now we must teach him the "*finish*", which is nothing more or less than bringing him once again to the "*Sit!*" position at your left side.

THE "FINISH"

Your dog, after the recall, is sitting facing you and you must bring him around, facing in the same direction you are, and to your left side. To do so requires usage of the leash again. Hold the slack in your left hand and place your right hand, palm down, on the leash

To execute the "Finish" the pupil must be brought behind the trainer and into the "Heel" position again. Illustrated is the first step.

The second step in the "Finish," bringing the dog behind the trainer so that the pupil can reach the "Heel" position at the trainer's left side.

between you and your dog and, by pressure with your right hand, pull the animal toward your right. As you do this step back with your right leg leaving your left foot and leg in the position it was, and give the command, "*Spike—Heel!*" As you guide the dog behind you, his muzzle facing toward your left side, pass the leash from one hand to the other, behind, then in front, ending with it in your right hand, meanwhile bringing your right leg back to its former position beside your left leg.

As soon as the dog has reached the heel position on your left side, give him the command to "*Sit!*" and the exercise is finished. This sounds much more complicated that it really is. Study the directions carefully for a few minutes, perhaps practice the movements without the dog so that you make no mistakes, and you will find the whole movement easy to execute.

Every breed has its natural limitations. This fine German Shepherd can do many jobs well, but it would be ridiculous to attempt to train him to point or course game.

Your pupil's collar and leash should symbolize the **rapport** that exists between you and your dog. This close understanding will soon extend beyond the training period.

Teaching the **"Down"**. Through the proper usage of hand, voice, and implied intention the Boxer has dropped to the correct position. If the dog does not obey promptly, stepping on the leash to force him down, as illustrated below, combined with hand signal and vocal command, conveys the message.

Make your pupil come to a definite "Sit" before you and "Sit-stay" until released by the "Heel" command and a gentle tug on the leash.

The hardest part is to coax the pupil to move to the right and around your right leg to pass behind you. The whole exercise must be executed smoothly and fluidly without any hitches or hesitations in between. Let me caution you not to give the "*Heel*" command in the "*finish*" too quickly. Allow the dog to sit in front of you for a few seconds before you issue the command for the "*finish*". If you don't condition him to a definite pause between the front "*Sit!*" and the "*Heel!*" to "*finish*", he will soon, of his own accord, eliminate the front "*Sit*", or give it only token recognition, and circle immediately into the "*Heel!*" position for the "*finish*".

COMMENTS

The hand signal I advocated earlier in this chapter for use during the "*Come!*" was merely an added means of coaxing your dog to break the "*Stay!*" command. Later I explained that a dog, called from a distance, might confuse a hand signal for one accompanying another command since canine vision is limited. I personally use the hand signal developed in Germany for the recall which, when combined with two other hand signals brings the "*finish*" to a neat close.

First use the oral command, "*King—Come!*" and, as the dog approaches you and reaches a point where his vision is clear and your movements easily seen by him, bring both palms up to your chest, elbows at your side, palms flat against your chest with fingers pointing upward toward your chin. Hit your chest with your palms to create a hollow sound as he comes in. Later, when he is letter perfect, you may eliminate the Tarzan beat and simply tap your chest with your palms.

Bringing the dog in to the "Sit" position before the "finish" when the animal is working off the leash. The author is using the hands-to-chest signal.

The correct deportment in reference to automobiles must be learned early by your dog in this era of fantastic and frightening traffic. Conditioning him to obey your commands promptly, both inside the car and out, can greatly diminish the possibility of a future accident.

Medium-sized to large dogs can be generally trained not to jump up on people by utilizing the knee-to-chest method, as shown in the photo. Below, the Afghan is being taught to walk at the **"Heel"** position by quick jerks on the lead to move him up into position and keep him walking briskly in the wanted direction.

With the dog heeding your palm-against-chest signal and therefore sitting before you, move you left hand, fingers pointing down, index finger extended, in a circling motion behind you, much as you moved your hand when you put pressure on the leash to bring him around you to the right for the "*finish*". Use the "*Heel!*" command with the hand motion.

When he has circled behind you and come to the "*Sit!*" position at heel at your left side, hold your left hand down, palm toward his nose, fingers extended and pointing toward the ground, in a stopping gesture directly in front of his face. To ulitize the last signal the leash must be passed from the left to the right hand.

By combining the visual (*hand*) and oral (*voice*) commands you

Three phases of the "recall" and "finish." First the dog (off leash) is called in to the trainer by the vocal command, "Come" augmented by the hand-to-chest signal (the trainer here using only one hand).

are conditioning your dog to obey either while, at the same time, bolstering and making more important, the basic vocal commands. Later, with your dog working off leash, you will not be burdened with this important implement to early training and your dog will, after awhile, react to only your hand signals, if you wish him to do so.

At left the Chow pupil has been brought in to the "Sit-stay" in front of the trainer and awaits the "Heel" command and signal to "finish." This dog, too, is working off leash. The trainer with the Boston has just completed the exercise and her dog, on leash, is at "Heel."

Performing "figure eights" between human obstacles brings greater performance sureness to your pupil.

CHAPTER 8

BASIC TRAINING COMPLETED

You and your pupil are now on the training homestretch. As a matter of fact if you were to quit now you would, for all general purposes, have a very well trained and behaved canine citizen.

But we are going to add a bit of extra polish to our pupil's basic education and teach him to "*Stand!*" and to "*Stand—stay!*" These commands, when learned, will help you to groom and wash your dog with greater ease and will be excellent training for the show ring should he prove to mature into a specimen of show caliber. This is also an exercise that is required in the obedience ring.

Many show people will tell you that it is not good to train your dog in obedience if you are going to show him. They seem to, after much questioning, object to the heeling-sit position which the trained animal takes when you come to a halt. With this new exercise we confound such objectors because we can, by giving the command, have the dog stand instead of sit. Another advantage found in training your dog to this "*Stand!*" command is in basic cleanliness during inclement weather. If you are walking your dog during rainy or snowy weather and you stop to chat with a neighbor or friend, the "*Stand-stay!*" command will keep your dog from sitting down in mud or water and soiling his underparts.

TEACHING TO "STAND-STAY!"

Take your usual starting position with the dog at "*Sit!*" beside you. Begin to move ahead giving the "*Heel!*" command then, as you come to the stop when your pupil ordinarily takes the "*Sit!*" position at your side, reach down quickly with your left hand, put it under his belly and hold him up (or keep him from sitting), issuing at the same time the command, "*Stand!*" If you have followed directions from the beginning of this book you will be aided in your endeavor by the early training you gave the puppy to stand while holding him at arm's length.

Once you have made the dog obey the "*Stand!*" command, bring your palm down before his face giving the command to "*Stay!*" and step away from him. His posture may be deplorable, but do not attempt to correct it until he is perfect in reacting to the "*Stand-stay!*" command.

At this stage of his training it is necessary to bring in a third party, namely someone who will oblige you by walking around the dog, touching him here and there, much as a show ring judge would do during examination in the conformation ring, while the animal, obeying your "*Stand-stay!*" command, stands rock-still.

When you return to the dog give him the "*Stand-stay!*" command again so he will remain standing. His tendency will be to sit as soon as you reach his side. In this exercise the leash should be handled as little as possible. Merely allow it to hang with a comfortable slack during the whole performance.

When the lesson is learned, circle around him when you return

The "Stand - stay" holds your dog in this position without moving while a stranger examines the pupil in the same manner as would a dog show judge.

The "Stand-stay," or "Stand for examination" is excellent discipline for your pupil. Note the loose leash as he stands to be examined.

as you did in the "*Sit-stay!*" and "*Down-stay!*" and touch him gently here and there. If he turns his head to look at you, push it back gently to face toward the front.

COMMANDS COMBINED

Again, as you always have done, go through the whole routine of commands. Be sure your dog differentiates between the "*Sit-stay!*" and the "*Stand-stay!*" If you have your pupil in the "*Sit-stay!*" at your side and wish to give him the command to "*Stand-stay!*" take a step or two forward to get him to a stand naturally before giving the command. About five sessions should perfect him.

Work with your dog, keeping the commands, and his conditioned reflexes to them, fresh. Take him with you when you go shopping or visiting so that he will learn to obey under different environmental circumstances.

After you are sure that your dog will obey any and all of the commands he has been taught by you smoothly and with perfection, then

Take your pupil with you wherever you go so that he will learn to obey quickly and without hesitation even in strange surroundings.

This French Bulldog has reached that desired goal in his training where he can be worked with confidence off-leash.

you must remove the leash and put him through the whole routine of exercises off leash and free.

WORKING OFF LEASH

When you begin *"Heeling!"* your dog off leash, if he is tall enough at the shoulder, it is best to at first loop one finger in the circle of the chain choke collar for physical control. Lessen this control until your pupil is *"Heeling!"* free, naturally and well.

Please do not rush into this phase of training. If you do you can very well ruin all that you have accomplished before. Be absolutely sure that your dog is ready to work off leash. If he still needs help on leash in any of the exercises or any small phase of them, he is not ready to work free. Your pupil must be an absolutely and completely reliable student on the leash before he can be allowed to work without it.

If possible it is the better part of valor to begin working your dog off leash in an enclosure where he can be easily captured should he

The signal to "Sit-stay" is given and the trainer prepares to leave the pupil. All of these training exercises are being performed off leash.

The dog is at the "Sit-stay" at a distance and being held in that position, awaiting a new command, by the hand signal of the trainer.

Here the trainer has just left the side of the pupil who is at the "Sit-stay" position.

Recalled from a distance the trainer is giving the "Down" hand signal and the dog has immediately quit his forward trot and dropped to the "Down" position.

The Boston Terrier is executing the long "Sit" off leash while, in the lower photograph, the author's two Shepherds perform the long "Down."

prove less reliable than you thought. You must act relaxed and pretend that the dog is on leash and as completely under your control as he was before. Any uneasiness on your part will be conveyed to your dog and reflect in his behavior.

Generally speaking, you will find that working *off* leash presents no more problems than working *on* leash and I am sure that if you have followed instructions faithfully you will be very proud of your trained dog.

Just one word of caution here. Often dogs will work with less vigor and punctuality off leash. Do not allow it. Make your dog work with all the snap and accuracy he exhibited when on leash. It is very easy for either you or your animal to fall into sloppy behavior once the major part of his basic training is over. Examine yourself first if your pupil has lost his early spark in performance. Perhaps it is your attitude that is the cause. If so, correct it, in both you and your dog.

If you have taught your dog and taught him well, by turning to Chapter 10 and reading the qualifications necessary for a dog to earn his C.D. degree in the Novice Class, you will be amazed to see that your dog is more than ready to compete. There is but one thing he will lack at this stage, that is the sense of competition that comes from working with other dogs and their handlers, and this you can rectify by entering an obedience class in your neighborhood.

Teaching your dog to jump is fun for both of
you and excellent exercise for the animal
who will later jump off-leash to retrieve objects which you throw.

CHAPTER 9

EXTRA TRAINING BONUSES

There are always a few more hints to give, a word or two more to say before talk on training is completed, advice that should be given about subjects not directly covered by general training, but important in canine deportment.

One of these yet to be spoken of problems is barking. Some dogs are noisy and bark at everything. It is their nature to do so, for they are members of a breed that is genetically noisy. Most owners want to control the barking of their dog so he will quit when told to do so. To accomplish this grasp the animal by the muzzle to hold his jaws together and give him the command, "*Quiet!*" uttered sharply. "*No!*" can also be used, but when you use it you are admonishing the dog for committing a misdemeanor and, in so doing you make him feel guilty for raising an alarm to protect you and your family and property. You want him to tell you when something is amiss or when someone is approaching. But you also want him to quit when he has done his duty and you give him the command to subside. For all these reasons the new command "*Quiet!*" is to be preferred to "*No!*" or "*Shame!*"

In an earlier chapter I promised to convey more information on how to break your dog of jumping up on your or you friends (who will soon be your enemies if this canine deportment continues). As your dog jumps up to plant his forefeet on your chest or thigh, according to his and your height, bring your knee up quickly into his chest to knock him off balance, at the same time sharply admonishing him with the "*No!*" command. A few repetitions of this form of correction should cure the culprit.

Your dog has learned the "*Halt!*" command during his training in

Another way of teaching your dog not to jump up on people. Your knee, raised and pushed into his chest, throws him off balance.

heeling. You will find that later the usefulness of this command can be broadened to bring to a stop any activity the dog may be engaged in at the moment that you wish halted immediately.

If the "*Halt!*" command is learned well it will aid you immeasurably in controlling a dog that is off leash, has become panicked, and is running away. Sometimes a familiar command that gets through the fog of fright to his consciousness will stop him and bring him back to a modicum of control.

There is a trick that German trainers use on dogs who persist in running wild or away when released from the leash, and it works with a sort of animal magic. The dog who engages in such conduct does so fully conscious of the fact that, once he has put distance between you, you cannot reach him to chastise him for his misconduct. The trick is to prove him wrong and to do this you must employ another chain choke collar which you will retain in your hand.

When the culprit has run off and heeds your commands to return not at all, you must throw the chain collar so that it strikes either very close to him or hits his hocks. His confident cockiness will fall immediately into shattered shards around him. You have done what he thought you were incapable of doing, reached him at a distance to punish him, and he will return on command, crestfallen and forever after in awe of your power.

Every dog should have his own area in the home. This is designated as his "place" and he should be trained to go to it when the command, "Place" is given him.

Retrieving thrown objects, such as the typical
training dumbbell, will give your dog needed
exercise and prepare him for the "fetch"
which is a part of more advanced training.

In the house every dog should have a place to call his own where his bed is and where he can snooze in peace. This area should be referred to as his "*Place!*" and when you want the rascal out from under your feet for any good and valid reason, the command "*Place!*" should send him scuttling to that spot of sanctuary to stay until called. To train him is simply a matter of identifying this location by pointing to it and repeating the word, "*Place!*" Later you can command, "*Fido, go to your PLACE!*" and he will obey.

Some dogs are forever carrying sticks or other objects in their mouths or bringing them to you. If your dog enjoys this form of entertainment it will be easy to teach him to "*Fetch!*" Repeat this command each time he brings anything to your hand. Or throw a stick or other object and command him to "*Fetch!*" it. Most dogs of the hunting breeds are easily taught this command as well as many individuals of other breeds. Later you can broaden this command to include the daily newspaper or your slippers, if you wish.

This Dachshund is retrieving a duck . . . indoors. The dog has been trained to "fetch" the duck as a part of an exhibition routine, a specialty trick his trainer was canny enough to recognize the Dachsie had a special aptitude to perform.

The broad jump, off-leash. Another training
bonus that will be of use later on if you
wish to continue to train your dog toward a
more advanced stage of learning.

Jumping is another fun thing that most dogs like to do. To train them to do it upon command requires only that you join them when they jump, taking them over the jump with you and issuing the command, "*Jump!*" or "*Hup!*" if you prefer. In no time at all you will be able to direct your dog toward an obstacle and he will sail over it at your command, like a veteran steeplechaser. This exercise in jumping will pay dividends later on if you wish to continue in obedience, particularly if you combine the object retrieving with the jumping (*see Open Class Competition, Obedience Trials, Chapter* 10).

You and your dog have now reached a point where you are a well-trained team. Take pride in your accomplishment and in the willingness and trainability of your dog that made your accomplishment as a trainer possible. I have given you all the necessary fundamentals to make training your dog as easy as possible and, to have reached this page and the corresponding stage in training that it represents, you have evidently used everything written here to the best of advantage. If you wish to indulge in advance training you and your dog have as fine a training base as is possible and you can go on to any areas of training (within genetic and physical limits) you wish. The interesting world of canine training is your oyster. Good luck!

There are training classes all over the country and there is probably one very near where you live where you can take your dog and, for a very nominal fee, work with other owners interested in training and obedience work.

CHAPTER 10

OBEDIENCE TRAINING AND TRIALS

Within the area of obedience trial competition there are match shows for the neophyte which are extremely interesting, will allow you to meet other dog owners who, like yourself, are interested in training, and give both you and your dog that first taste of competition, but in an easy-to-take fashion. If you are lucky (or competent) you may also win a small (but always cherished) trophy in these informal matches. Such competitions will probably whet your appetite for more exciting and difficult obedience trials such as those which are held all over the country under the auspices of the American Kennel Club. These trials are divided into four classes. You perform under a judge who scores your dog according to its ability to perform the various exercises. There are four classes in these obedience trials: Novice, Open, Utility, and Tracking.

OBEDIENCE TRIAL CLASSES: NOVICE

The dog will be judged on the following point basis for his performance.

Test	Maximum Score
Heel on leash	35
Stand for examination by judge	30
Heel free—off leash	45
Recall (come upon command)	30
One minute sit	30
Three minute down	30
Maximum total score	200

The dog must *"qualify"* by earning at least 50 percent of the points for each test with a total of 170 points out of a possible 200 points for each trial, and he must do this in three different shows. If he is successful he is entitled to wear the C.D. title after his name as an indication that he has earned his Companion Dog degree. There is also competition for trophies at these shows which are awarded to the highest scoring animals. This holds true for all classes of obedience competition.

OPEN CLASS COMPETITION

The dog is eligible for Open Class competition only after he has qualified as a Companion Dog (C.D.)

Following is the basis upon which your dog is judged in Open Class competition.

Take advantage of special apptitudes your dog may have. This owner realized that her Pug liked to jump through things and soon had the little fellow jumping through a ring formed by her arms.

"All work and no play . . . etc." So remember to have some playtime with your pupil even if his name is not Jack. This also helps him to recognize the difference between the training session and funtime.

Test	Maximum Score
Heel free	40
Drop on recall	30
Retrieve (*wooden dumbell*) on flat	25
Retrieve (*wooden dumbell*) over hurdle	35
Broad jump	20
Three minute sit (*handler out of sight*)	25
Five minute down (*handler out of sight*)	25
Maximum total score	200

As before in the Novice Class, the dog must qualify in three shows before being eligible for the Companion Dog Excellent (C.D.X.) degree, which is a most difficult test of both your training skill and your dog's ability to learn, but not nearly as difficult as those to come.

UTILITY DOG DEGREE

After your dog has been awarded his C.D.X. he is eligible to compete in Utility Dog Competition. To enter here he must be, of necessity, a very finished performer as perusal of the tests involved will show.

Test	Maximum Score
Scent discrimination (*selecting and picking up article handled by trainer from group of articles—Article #1*)	20
Scent discrimination—Article #2	20
Scent discrimination—Article #3	20
Seek back (*finding and retrieving article dropped by handler*)	30
Signal exercises (*all familiar training exercises executed by dog from hand signals only*)	35
Directed jumping (*Over hurdle and bar*)	40
Group examination	35
Maximum total score	200

Success in three trials in Utility Dog Competition earns the dog the coveted U.D. title.

TRACKING TEST

To enter a tracking test your animal's tracking ability must first be observed and approved for competition by a licensed tracking judge. Then in order to qualify, the dog must follow the trail laid

A great deal of satisfaction can be derived from Obedience Trial competition. Your dog is scored on performance alone and a really good and well-trained animal, like this Weimaraner, can score high and take his share of trophies.

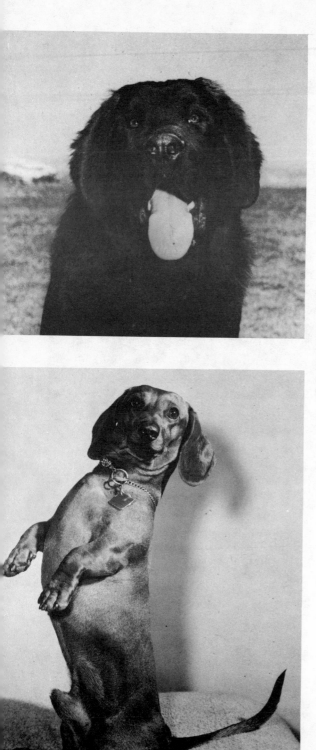

The breed you choose to own and train does not matter. Though some breeds seem to have a greater aptitude for training, all dogs can be trained to be good canine citizens.

by a strange person, under specified conditions, in competition with at least three other dogs and under the observation of two A.K.C. qualified tracking judges.

Tracking tests are generally held separately from other obedience competition. The dog works on a long lead held by his handler and must be trained to the Nth. degree to qualify. Usually dogs go into the Tracking competition with their U.D. degree and, if they qualify for the Tracking Dog. (T.D.) title, simply add the T. after the U.D. making the full title, Utility Dog, Tracker (U.D.T.).

Those of you who are inclined to go on in obedience work and reap the very real rewards that come from accomplishment in this most rugged competition, as well as the trophies, ribbons, and cash awards, should write to The American Kennel Club, 51 Madison Avenue, New York City, 10010, and ask them to send you their free booklet "Regulations and Standards for Obedience Trials".

If you become truly earnest about obedience work and go all out in the toughest Obedience Trial competition and advanced work, then make certain that your dog is capable of learning all you wish to teach him, that he is willing to learn and is physically able to perform the exercises necessary. If he isn't, then be content with simply a well trained dog and, for the tough Obedience trial competition, get yourself another dog that will meet all the requirements necessary to make him a top flight contender in the most difficult area of canine competition . . . The Obedience trial.

THE END

INDEX